Gladys Hunt's "How-to" Handbook

for inductive Bible study leaders

(formerly It's Alive!)

Harold Shaw Publishers
Wheaton, Illinois 60187

Contents

Foreword

For twenty years small group Bible studies have given sparkle to my personal spiritual life, enhanced my witness to others and allowed me to participate in the great things God is doing in the world.

I write this book with strong conviction because I have a life full of miracle stories from all kinds of studies in all sorts of places. The study of God's Word provides a basic, solid foundation for becoming an intelligent, believing Christian, and I have seen more people enter God's family by this means than any other.

I am deeply indebted to Inter-Varsity Christian Fellowship for years of training and experience. Inter-Varsity is more than a university student movement; it is a way to think about God and the authority of Scripture in daily life. It was during my student days that I was first encouraged to handle the Bible with integrity and unleash its message to my friends.

Gladys M. Hunt
Ann Arbor, Michigan

1

God's Placement Bureau

New neighbors had moved in next door when we returned from a summer away from home. From the beginning I found Leslie my kind of person. She was easy to know and her conversation was stimulating. Almost daily we discussed the state of the world, our own new ideas, and things we had read about.

As our friendship developed, I invited her to join our Bible study. She was a thoughtful person and I felt confident she would enjoy investigating the spiritual dimensions of life. When she accepted the invitation, I suggested that she might like to do some homework before the next study. We were studying *Romans*. Would she like to read it before coming, since we were already well into the book?

I left with her a modern English version of

Romans to make easier reading of such a doctrinal book, and she dug into it with her typical enthusiasm. Only days later she called to say that she had read the book of *Romans* through twice. When could I come over? She had so many questions!

And what questions she had! She began by checking out her understanding of how a person gets a right standing before God—what it means to be justified. Her questions involved original, eager insights into what the text was saying. She said, "Paul contradicts himself. In one place he says whoever calls on the name of the Lord will be saved; in another he speaks of God choosing people. Which is right?"

We talked for a long time about how both ideas are part of the Christian message. Jesus said, "No one comes to me unless the Father draws him," and "He who comes to me I will not cast out." It was a scary idea to her.

Then Leslie told me that many years ago when she was a student she had heard a speaker present this message at her sorority house. She had been attracted to Jesus Christ then and had had long conversations with the speaker about knowing God and, as far as she knew, she thought she had given her life over to Jesus Christ then. But the in-between years produced no new growth and the initial feeling had faded. Still, she had been restless all these years, as if she'd had a glimpse through a doorway at something uniquely different—as if she knew life held more than she was experiencing. And now God had put her next door to us so she could become personally involved with him again.

I listened with awe and finally said, "Leslie, I think the Father is drawing you."

She replied with the same wonder that I felt. "Oh, Rusty, so do I."

A year has passed since then. Today as I sat in our neighborhood Bible study with Leslie—a new study which she initiated—a large feeling came over me. Almost goose bumps. I thought of the eternal dimensions of what had happened. This kind of adventure with our heavenly Father lifts life out of the ordinary.

We *are* in on something big when we link our lives up with him. God even knows who to put in the house next door. I can never quite get used to the marvel of that, and yet over the years I have learned to live expectantly. I think of the places I have lived—none of them without purpose when I opened my eyes and let God direct me. In my life this stretching experience began a long time ago.

I was a college sophomore living on the second floor of Mason Hall when the Inter-Varsity staff worker visited me in my room. After talking with me about the dynamics of my personal relationship with God, she began to ask about my roommates and the other students who lived in my hall. Questions like: What are their interests? How well do you know them? Have you seen any evidence that God is drawing any of them to himself?

Frankly, up until this time, I thought I had been doing pretty well to survive as a Christian at a big university, develop some friendships and get satisfactory grades in my course work. But she was after something more. She suggested that God had put me in *my* dormitory, on *my* floor, in *my* room by divine design. In God's economy I had not simply been programmed by a large impersonal university machine. I was involved in a larger plan than that. "God places his children carefully," she said, "and perhaps you will be the first Christian many of them have ever met."

Encouraging me to be expectant, she gave me some instruction on the how-to of starting a dorm Bible study. And then she left. I didn't see her again that year, but she had given me enough vision to last a long time.

I decided to capitalize on all those good bull-sessions we had over cheese and crackers in our room. Religion was a topic we always got to sooner or later, and I had found real freedom in discussing my Christian convictions with the regulars from down the hall who gathered in our room. I hadn't recognized it before, but surely among these were individuals in whose heart God had already begun to work. How could I have been so blind!

Out of this came the first Bible study I ever led. Probably it was poorly done. I was undoubtedly over-anxious to prove what the Bible was saying. My discussion questions were home-made, without experience. In brief, it probably wasn't good from any technical point of view. But it was the Word of God which was unleashed in a room full of women students, and it was alive!

Most of them had never read it before and as I saw God take his truth and apply it to people with half a dozen different backgrounds, I began to believe new things about the Word of God being a sword. I saw eternal Truth touch the lives of my friends. And, as importantly for me, the book I had taken for granted became the living Word—authoritative, corrective and the revelation of Life.

By so simple a thing as inviting my friends to study the Bible with me I was in on something bigger than I had ever known before. But it wasn't just seeing what the Bible, opened and discussed, could do in our lives; it was coming to grips with the way God works in the world.

While I made plans to go to the housing office early to get the extra spacious corner room in a new dormitory for next fall, God was weaving together another design and preparing a place of ministry for me. I saw it happen throughout my university days. There are no "no vacancies" with God. I have a healthy respect for God's placement department as I look back over my life.

It's an exciting moment of truth to find out that God has put you in your house, in your apartment, on your street, in your town with an eternal plan in mind. It totally transforms the nuisance of inadequate urban planning, noise, pollution, and even the strangeness of a new town.

In the excitement of getting married after graduation from the university, I forgot about how practical God is in making plans for us. God gave us a spacious first home, and I selfishly thought he put us there just for us. It took me a while to see he always has more in mind than just making us cozy. When we made our second move, I told the realtor I didn't like stucco houses. Furthermore, we decided we would live in any town along a certain commuter line, except one. You guessed it! We bought a stucco house in that town. It turned out again to be God's good idea.

In a day when our society is increasingly mobile, some families move very often. Tearing up roots and moving on can be a traumatic series of worries about whether the living room will hold the furniture, whether the payments are too high, whether the school system is good enough—and myriads of other temporal problems. But when we trust a sovereign God he goes ahead and prepares a place. He *does* have a design which involves eternity.

Look at your neighborhood with new eyes—whether you've lived there for twenty years or two months. Is there any evidence that God has put you there with a purpose in mind?

I was talking one day with Judy, a student who lived on a huge university campus. She had been praying for her whole dorm, asking God to cause students who lived there to turn to him. It was a vague, large prayer. Remembering my own experience, I suggested that she look closer to "home." Who lived in the next room? Who lived in her hall? Might God already be working in some of these? We prayed, asking God to open Judy's eyes to see them.

She called me excitedly the next day. Pat, a girl who lived two rooms down the hall, regularly stopped by and ate up Judy's time talking about nothing. She was a nuisance as far as Judy was concerned. She usually dropped in at an inconvenient time and stayed too long. She was there again that afternoon and seemed her usual purposeless self. Judy said,

"Suddenly, as if my eyes were newly opened, I saw Pat, not as a nuisance, but as God must see her. I didn't have to develop contacts for him. I already had one in Pat. I began to steer the conversation to speak about a meaningful life. I heard myself asking, 'Pat, have you ever trusted Jesus Christ?' And her answer really got to me. She said, 'How can you trust somebody you don't know?' "

When Judy suggested that Jesus could be known by studying one of the Gospels, Pat eagerly accepted the invitation. They had begun a study that very afternoon and were planning to invite others from their hall the next day.

It's easy to "care" for a whole town, a whole continent, or the people who live across town. It's not so easy to look on our block or in our own apartment building. That is, until we catch hold of the idea that God has placed us where we are with a purpose in mind. And finding that purpose makes life sing!

When we think seriously about it, it does seem a bit ludicrous to appear before the Lord, rejoicing in the redeemed from other lands for whom we prayed and sent the message, while never having shared the Good News with the people who live next door. But that happens all too frequently when we are arrogant enough to believe that *we* found *our* house or *our* apartment or *our* room and fail to recognize that the great General knows how to place his troops.

So there I was? married and settled. Dormitory Bible studies were something I knew about. I had pragmatic evidence that this was a good way to reach people with God's truth. I couldn't see why the same thing wouldn't work in a neighborhood. All it would take was a few interested people who wanted to know what the Bible said. The technique is really both simple and profound. We ask three kinds of questions of the text:

What does it say? *find facts*
What does it mean? *interpret*
What does it mean to me? *apply*

No teacher is needed. We dig into the text together and discover what it is saying. I guess it never occurred to me that a group of people who could read and think couldn't have a profitable time together this way.

I fell into my first neighborhood Bible study quite without realizing what was happening. I had met another young mother, a pretty, shining woman who was already the mother of children aged three and two, and pregnant again. In the course of conversation I discovered she had only recently become a believer in Christ and felt quite shaky about all that was involved in living the Christian life. Some weeks later I heard that she had delivered twins! That meant four children, aged three and under.

It didn't take much wisdom to realize that she would need encouragement. So I went to call on Denise, taking with me my own small child. She greeted me from a mound of diapers that needed folding next to a sink full of dirty dishes. We folded diapers together, swept up the lint, and demolished the dirty dishes. Then, before leaving for home, I suggested we read something from the Bible together and pray. Her spirits lifted noticeably as the dimension of God came into her rather overwhelming situation. She asked if I would come again the next week to read and pray with her.

I went the next week, and the next. And it became obvious that the encouragement came from reading the Bible together, not from folding diapers. Some weeks later, when she had her life more in hand, she suggested inviting her neighbor in to read and discuss the Bible with us. I brought my friend, Jane, with me to share in the excitement of what we were discovering. Denise's neighbor came, and then another and another. Women who were encountering a whole new point of view about life knew of others down the street who could profit by coming. Soon we had a room full of young mothers and thrice as many children meeting each week.

What a motley group we were! No church, some church, liberal church, Catholic church—and others scared to death of God. We used discussion questions, found our answers in the text of the Bible, and great things began to happen.

One of the nicest of these was the ministry of two older women who enjoyed working with children. They heard of the size of the Bible study and of the vast confusion we endured in trying to keep eighteen children quiet in the recreation room each week. They volunteered to take care of the children, and not only kept them happy, but brought handcrafts, flannelgraph stories and songs about Jesus into their lives.

I guess I'll really never know all that happened in that neighborhood because of that Bible study. Each year some families moved away and new people moved in and joined the study group. I moved away myself sixteen years ago, but the Bible study still goes on in that same neighborhood. What a large thing a little visit became. It was no accident that I was once taught to look strategically at my dormitory. And it was no accident that I lived in that town and met Denise.

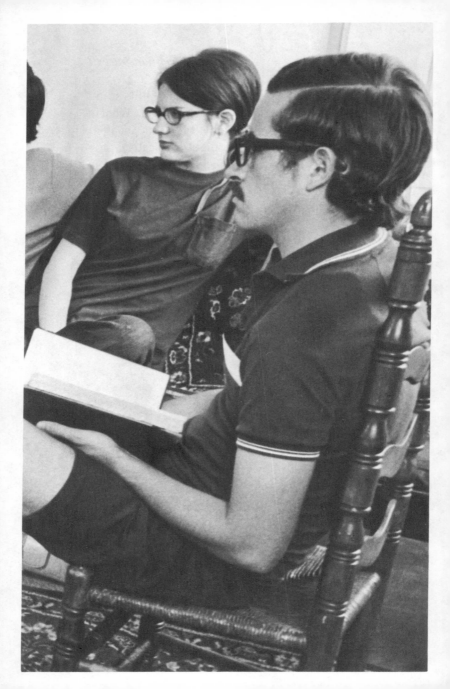

**Start a
Bible study?
Help!**

Already I can hear some of you say, "I could never do it!"

And probably you never will if you concentrate on *you.* That's why I began with the idea of the divine placement of God. Surely he wouldn't put you in a needy place and then expect you to handle the situation all by yourself? That's what trusting God is all about. He's already at work in *your* world. You have to decide whether the Bible is true in a personal, practical way when it says, "When he calls you, he will enable you."

The secret is having an adequate view of God—in letting him be who he really is—in your life. Most of life's problems are solved by a right view of God. People get in the habit of playing it safe, of never going out on the limb with God. No wonder they have a shrivelled view of him. They've kept themselves in a closet away from him. Saying *I couldn't possibly do it* is a statement about us, not about God. And it's that God-dimension in our lives that makes the difference.

Whenever I hear someone say, "I don't have enough faith," I think of atrophied muscles. Faith isn't a commodity one collects and stores in a drawer to be pulled out at appropriate needy moments. Faith is *now*. It is a dynamic principle of life. It is believing God. It is linking your life up with him, daring to believe that he can do through you more than you've ever dreamed possible.

How does a person get more faith? *By beginning to exercise what little he has.* That's the first and biggest hurdle. In the area of initiating a Bible study, the first hurdle is inviting someone to study the Scripture with you. That can be a scary idea. What if you're turned down? What if someone thinks you're a religious kook?

It isn't as risky as it sounds when you actually get involved. Pray for one contact, one good conversation that can lead into spiritual things. Ask God to open your eyes to see people who are really eager to know what the Bible says. You will be surprised at what he will do. And your faith will spring up like new grass in spring rain.

I know this works because I've tried it myself and I keep hearing of others who are having this kind of an alive experience with God. Dr. Sanford, a university professor in Colorado, and his wife were concerned about involving other faculty members and their wives in a discussion study of the Scriptures. They invited a colleague and his wife over for dinner one night, and before they knew what was happening they heard the fellow professor say, "What's all this interest you have in the Bible? I feel left out. My wife goes to a study with your wife and I never get a chance to participate. How about us studying something from the Bible together tonight?"

Hardly anyone expects that kind of answer to prayer. It cancels all the planned speeches, lets the adrenalin supply to the blood drain off, and leaves the supplicant totally disarmed. And I think a great omnipotent God smiles and says, "See?"

A second hurdle involves the leadership of the study. You don't have to be a teacher. You don't need a year at Bible school or a seminary degree. Nor do you have to teach the group. The kind of Bible study I'm talking about *provides an opportunity to ask rather than to tell.* The Bible will do the telling. Using good discussion questions, we investigate together what the text is saying. A small relaxed group together discussing the Scripture—with the Holy Spirit as the teacher. Do you have a God big enough to accomplish that?

When Jesus walked by the Sea of Galilee over nineteen hundred years ago he called simple fishermen to him and said, "Follow me, and I will make you fishers of men." They left their nets and followed him. These men knew the excitement of the catch. And they knew Jesus could involve them in something far bigger than catching fish. Our difficulty is that we have forgotten the excitement of the catch, if indeed we ever knew it. The sheer adventure of seeing truth dawn in the heart of another person and change his life is an experience without parallel. No one is ever quite the same after having a part in this kind of adventure.

Usually it comes in rather simple packages, not the stuff out of which headlines are made. For instance, Bonnie came to our Bible study at the invitation of another woman who had just found her life's restless yearning met by Jesus Christ. Bonnie's husband had a bad reputation in the town and his associations made her feel like a moral leper. She was obviously ill at ease. I was surprised to see her at the study. Every week she came but she never spoke. She always sat in the same chair, never raising her head, her eyes glued to the Bible in her lap. The weeks went by and then Bonnie's head began to come up. She dared to look furtively at the others in the room. More weekly studies. Bonnie began to relax. The day she participated in the study—actually making a good observation about the text—was like a sunrise for all of us. It was like being in on a miracle in a woman's heart—a miracle that was only just beginning. That's the kind of excitement I'm talking about, and it's hard to define. It's the "catch" Jesus was talking about, and it's exciting because it involves a person and eternity.

Because those disciples followed Jesus, you and I can know Jesus Christ today. If you had asked any of them if they felt capable or qualified, you know what their answer would have been. They were an unlikely group—unlearned, untraveled, unread. What they had was a great personal experience with Jesus that was convincing. And Jesus committed the good news about God's redemption into their fumbling hands.

From a human point of view, that was a risk of cosmic proportions. How did heaven's planning council ever dare come up with an idea like that? The angels must have shaken their heads in holy wonder. Yet it's the beauty of redemption. Jesus said, "If a man loves me, I will come and make my home in him," thereby describing the ministry of the Holy Spirit. *God in us!*

Paul later wrote with the same kind of reckless confidence. He spoke of believers being "entrusted with the Gospel." As a missionary he visited a city, preached the Word of God, instructed the converts, established the church—and left them with the sacred trust. They were stewards. The Gospel was their responsibility. They must share it. He later wrote to the church at Thessalonica, "The message about the Lord went out from you not only to Macedonia and Greece, but news of your faith in God has gone everywhere."

They didn't have witnessing seminars in the first century church. They simply had a great experience with God and a strong confidence in the work of the Holy Spirit. And the Word of God was spread abroad by the believers.

Today in your neighborhood, in your office, or wherever God has put you, the Gospel is your responsibility. The good news about God is in your hands.

But by some strange quirk in history, the church has developed laymen who think the Gospel belongs to the professionals. They are often quick to say, "I couldn't possibly do that," never realizing that what they are really saying is, "I don't believe *God* could help me do that."

By an even stranger set of priorities, we fill our schedule with an assortment of temporal goals, as if being a trust officer for the truth of God were a very small thing.

We suffer from a low expectation of the life of God in men and a low view of God's power.

So before you say, "What, *me* start a Bible study?" read on. God may be saying to you in a fresh way, "Follow me!"

At this point you may be hesitant to ask the next unsettling question, *Are people really interested in Bible study?* Yes. Oh, not everyone, but enough to give all of us more than enough to do.

Jan recently moved to a new part of the city.

She had enjoyed a Bible study in her former neighborhood and wanted to begin one like it in her new location. She spent the summer developing friendships and when school began she invited the neighbors in to discuss the idea. The response was good and a study began.

The interaction within the group was so stimulating that Jan found herself talking about the Bible Study later that day with a mother from her daughter's class who stopped by on an errand. She had no idea what the woman's response would be, but when she finished explaining what they had done, the woman said wistfully, "I think that's wonderful. I've just bought a Bible and I have no one to read it with." You aren't surprised, are you, to hear that Jan was quick to invite her to join their group?

Surprises like this happen all the time to people who are expectant, who believe God is working. But some of us get too comfortable in our Christianity. We go way inside the rooms of the kingdom of God and find a comfortable place to sit down. The fellowship is so interesting there. And in our ease we forget that there are others groping outside the door, trying to find the way in. We forget to stand near the door to welcome people, to help them find the latch that opens the way to eternal life.

A paratroop instructor said that there are four commands he gives his parachutists: *Attention!*

Stand in the door. Look up. Follow me.

I think I hear the Lord Jesus giving those same commands to believers today.

**The
joy of
discovery**

Elaine, one of the town socialites, had come to our Wednesday morning Bible study for the first time. She was defensive at first as if she really didn't need this sort of thing but had come out of a magnanimous spirit to please the friend who invited her. But she was soon disarmed by the love which seems to characterize small group Bible studies, and then she was free to be herself.

We were studying John's Gospel—my favorite book for beginning small groups because it reveals so much about the Lord Jesus Christ.* Most of the women in the study had never read this Gospel before and thus were meeting Jesus and the woman at the well for the first time.

*Eyewitness: John's View of Jesus, 24 inductive studies in John's Gospel, is available through Harold Shaw Publishers.

A member of the group read the fourth chapter of John aloud; the rest followed along, engrossed in this marvelous conversation between Jesus and the Samaritan woman. When the reading was finished a breathless kind of sigh revealed our involvement in this encounter. Elaine said in a quiet, puzzled way, "Never thirst again? Never thirst again. What a promise to make!"

Another woman said, "Jesus makes it sound so satisfying."

"What does that mean—when Jesus says he can give living water?" asked another.

The discussion about the text had begun before the leader had a chance to initiate the first discussion question from the study guide. So she simply added a question here and there to keep the discussion centered on the text, making sure that all the points in the questions had been covered by the group. The contributions, the insights, the teaching, the convictions came from the Holy Spirit, who was obviously present to guide the group into the truth. It was awesome to hear what the women were discovering and the conclusions they were drawing about the person of Jesus.

As the study hour came to a conclusion Elaine remarked, "You know, I've been thinking. When that woman changed the subject and asked Jesus that question about where to worship—he could have answered all her religious questions and it wouldn't have helped her one bit. She had to face her sin before Jesus could help her." She paused and then added, "I need to do the same thing."

Elaine has been a Bible study regular since that day. More important than that, however, is her open membership in the family of God. And, as an extra happiness to finish the story, her mother and father have come to trust Jesus Christ through the witness of her life.

The main point in sharing not only Elaine's story, but the group experience in John 4 is to highlight the way the truths in that chapter entered the hearts of the group members. *They discovered living truth for themselves with the Holy Spirit's help.*

We could have had a Bible teacher, a professional, an expert come and tell us all about John 4. But while he (or she) was talking, some of our thoughts might have wandered or we might have missed the point, or just switched our minds into neutral. The delight of a functioning small group Bible study is that it has one hundred percent participation. There is a commitment to group involvement before each person ever comes. This is not a spectator sport; everyone gets into the action.

And participation means that individuals have the *joy of discovery*! A truth found for oneself is more really one's own than a truth heard from someone else. Discovering it, opening your mouth and verbalizing it—these acts make truth your own in a way that becomes part of you. We forget ninety percent of what we hear; we retain ninety percent of what we say.

You've had the experience, as I have, of sharing some great truth with someone and pontificating on it with such finesse that you are sure it will profoundly affect the other person. Only to have them share with you a week or two months later a wonderful thing they have discovered—and it's that great truth you already told them! And you want to say, "I told you that last week or last month," (but you're smart enough not to say anything). What happened? *They discovered it for themselves.*

I emphasize this not to exclude the place of the teaching of the Word of God by qualified people, but to compensate for a terrible neglect in the Christian world. We have acted as if the Holy Spirit could not teach an individual unless some human guardian and teacher of truth were present. We have developed pewsitters who are talked at year after year. Very few become participants in the arena of sharing the Word. After a lifetime of sitting under good preaching (or bad, as the case may be) people still say, "I just don't feel capable." *When it comes to handling the Scripture,* Paul wrote to a young man named Timothy, *you should learn how to use it aright.* John wrote to first century Christians and said that the Holy Spirit was in them and that they didn't need anyone to teach them because he would guide them into truth.

God's Word is alive and full of truth. When it is read with serious intent, the Holy Spirit enlightens people's minds and truth penetrates. We do not need a "pope" when we have the Holy Spirit, but sometimes we act as though we do.

A small group Bible study gives people an opportunity to open the Bible in a neutral environment and discuss what it says. It provides a natural bridge to inquire into spiritual issues, to consider the meaning of life, the person of Jesus Christ. Instead of telling your friends, you invite them to discover with you what the Bible says. It is not a preaching opportunity; it is a cooperative adventure in discovery. *Natural* is the best word to describe the kind of friendship and discussion that comes out of Bible study.

The idea of a Bible study is not unlike the idea of the popular Great Books studies available in some communities. Only in this case, the Great Book is the Bible. The principles for study are the same, only of larger import. We ask *What does it say*? and "fact" questions are the most important questions in the study. People like to jump into interpretation without getting the facts. A good study gets the facts clearly in mind. It takes the text seriously. This eliminates too many "I think" or "It seems to me" statements which have no basis for truth.

Then we ask *What does it mean*? We interpret

the facts so that we understand their significance. We are studying God's revelation to men. We *must* talk about the meaning of the facts because the ideas we are handling are life-changing.

When the facts are clear and the interpretation relevant to the facts, then we need only a few application questions. We should already have been "clobbered" with the truth.

These are the elements of any good study. The discussion questions will fall into one of those three categories. We weigh the facts, interpret them and come to a conclusion. This is called *inductive study.* You may think this a dull title, but it is an exciting process.

It's exhilarating because we don't have to be a profound persuader of men, a preacher or a prophet. We can simply be friends who believe God has spoken in a book. We read it together; we are judged together by its truth; our misconceptions are cleared up; sufficient information is imparted to lead to intelligent commitment.

Our friends, neighbors, co-workers are generally biblically illiterate (as we often are ourselves) and don't mind admitting this. The only qualification necessary for this kind of study is the belief that the Bible is worth studying. This is not for experts, but for people who want to investigate and discover together. But we *do* assume the importance of what the Bible says.

Jesus used the principles of inductive study in

his ministry. He used questions to involve his
hearers, to help them think through the issues involved. We are often hesitant about this idea of
Bible study because we think someone has to be
the answer man, the one who knows everything—
and we're scared that might turn out to be us. But
our *answer* is the text of the Bible. The questions
we use are intended to help us dig out truth. The
truth will be in the text.

If someone asks a question in the study not
covered by the text, "I don't know" is a perfectly
good answer for any group member to give. It
doesn't mean that an answer can't be found; it
simply means that it is not resolved in this text.
Further illumination may come later.

Then, somewhere along the line we got the idea
that if you were going to be the agent for starting
a Bible study, you'd have to know all the answers
before you begin. (That's a clever strategy Satan
put into operation.) No, you operate as peers—on
the same level—as you go to the Scripture together
as a group to find the answer. What is needed in a
leader is eagerness to hear the word of the Lord.

I am often astounded at the enthusiasm of new
Christians to begin Bible studies, and the para-
doxical fear of older Christians who believe they
could never do it! It almost convinces me that new
Christians believe God speaks through the Bible
more strongly and clearly than older Christians do.
(Is this because older Christians have sat under fine

preachers who speak of struggling over the text in preparing this sermon, who make it sound as if you have to know Greek and Hebrew and every cross reference to understand? Intimidated by the minister's skill and scholarship, the congregation comes to believe it cannot read the Bible and understand it.)

The most logical thing in the world, as far as Nancy was concerned, was for her to begin a Bible study on her street after she became a Christian. She needed to know what the Bible said; she was enthused every day by what she read; she was sure it would help her neighbors. With far less anxiety than those who had grown used to being Christians, she invited her neighbors and began rotating the leadership of the study, (a principle discussed in the next chapter.)

She said to me only recently, "I think the Bible is the neatest book I ever studied. God speaks to me right where I am living. And sharing all the ideas together makes it so much plainer to me."

When she takes her turn to lead the study she is so eager from all she has learned that she can hardly wait for everyone else to discover it, too. After the study she expresses amazement at how much the others taught her. Talk about the joy of discovery? She knows what it's about and calls it "neat."

One day when I went to the study that met in our neighborhood, I arrived to find that only three

of us had come that day. It was my turn to lead
the discussion and I was anxious to have others
find what I had discovered in my careful prepara-
tion. Now I was disappointed. It was too good a
chapter for the others to miss. During the study
the telephone rang and the hostess left the room
to answer it. While she was gone, Barbara, the only
other person left, quickly asked me, "I've been
wanting to ask you, do you think Jesus is saying
he is God? I've read and read these first chapters
this week, and I am sure that must be what he is
saying. What do you think?"

Then I knew why it was a small study that day.
Barbara was having the joy of personally discovering an overwhelming fact; the Holy Spirit was convincing her heart. She didn't want to risk stupidity
in front of the large group, but it was safe to ask
one other person. "Yes," I said, "I am sure that's
what Jesus is saying." And I later saw that discovery implemented in Barbara's life.

I've been enthused about this kind of study for
years, and in the course of knowing me many of
my friends have been subjected to enthusiastic
conversations about this way of sharing the
Gospel.

When my friend Natalie moved out into a beautiful posh area of the city, her mission field became the wives of young executives who lived all
around her. Spurred on by my enthusiasm she decided to try a neighborhood Bible study. Only she

was scared, too scared to try the idea of group leadership. So she looked for a capable friend who would lead it each time—discussion style, using the inductive method. It went well; the women were eager; they shared their problems, doubts and beliefs; they were honest and open. God was teaching them on their level of understanding.

Then the special leader friend moved away and Natalie had to do something. So instead of believing in her own "priesthood" as a believer, and trusting the Holy Spirit's ability to guide this group of peers into truth, she decided to invite a minister, noted for his Bible teaching ministry, to come and *teach* the group.

At first they were thrilled at this learned man's lectures. Then one young woman timidly tried asking a question. It was a simple thing, and by the way he answered the question she realized it was probably something she should have known. She was embarrassed. After that, no one asked any more questions. Neither was anyone ever asked to examine the text and come up with a conclusion. And they wouldn't have anyway because they didn't want to look stupid in front of someone who knew so much.

From the outside the group looked successful for a while. A group of Christian women from outside the neighborhood heard that the Reverend was teaching at Natalie's house and they came each week, swelling the attendance considerably.

But one by one the neighbors dropped out. Their excuses sounded legitimate each time, but too late Natalie realized that what she had each week was a house full of Christian women, thrilled again to be worshipful spectators listening to the biblical wisdom of a good lecturer.

You may dismiss this idea and label me anti-clerical or anti-church. I am not. We need capable expositors of the Bible multiplied a thousand fold. We need thousands of pulpits in our country where the Scripture is proclaimed with clarity and authority.

But having said that, we still need to get at the people who need to hear the message. They work and live in the areas where believers work and live. The people most likely to reach them are their peers. We cannot push our responsibility to witness off on the minister. And the best way to reach them is by exposing them to a honest investigation of what the Bible says about God, about man, about redemption. People need *content* to decide.

All of us know week-day studies where a hundred people—non-Christians and Christians—gather to hear a capable teacher. We like the successful sound of that kind of arrangement. Large numbers, a good teacher, and the satisfactory feeling of ministry for the teacher. And while I have no complaint against this kind of ministry, it does have obvious drawbacks if this is the only kind of Bible study ever encouraged.

Look at Natalie's neighborhood, for instance. If Natalie had believed that God teaches through the Bible and would use her influence in group leadership, she would have grown more spiritually vigorous herself. Furthermore, the study would have been more personal. A neighborhood grouping lends itself to sharing and honesty because it is small and safe, far less scary than an unfamiliar church and congregation. The environment would have prompted an openness about doubts and questions that are important to get cleared away. She would have had daily opportunities to enter dialogs about God with her neighbors.

Furthermore, how many more people could have been reached if the Christians who clustered to hear the minister teach would have each stayed in their own neighborhoods and reached five others? It's strategy and growth that I am talking about. The church is plagued with guilt over its silence; it is time to act where we live and work.

Again, let me repeat: there is a place for good biblical teaching. I am talking about something different—and it involves you inviting your friends, your neighbors, your co-workers into the joy of discovery through small group Bible studies.

**Teaching
one
another**

It was another Bible study group in another town. As I was getting ready to leave the house, I prayed that God would make this morning fresh and meaningful to me. We would be studying John 3. How many times since I was a little girl had I heard John 3 read, discussed, studied, preached about! No one needed to tell me that it was one of *the* most important chapters in the Bible, but it felt old and worn out as I thought about studying it again this day.

Arriving at the study I looked at our group. There was a grandmother present who had walked with God for years and had never lost her excitement over knowing him. Dena was a new, radiant Christian, and most of the non-Christians there were present because of her enthusiasm about

Jesus Christ. Phyllis was also a Christian, a fragile kind of believer, whose spiritual life had many ups and downs. Five others were at various levels of understanding what Jesus Christ was all about, mostly open and honest. One woman was holding onto her self-righteousness pretty tightly and only admitted to the beautiful sentiments in Jesus' words.

No two of us were alike in background, in temperament or in experience. Yet a miracle was going to take place. God was going to take the truth of one potent chapter recorded in the Bible and use it as a sword in each life to accomplish a specialized task in the individuals there. For some it would be "evangelism" because they would be comprehending the idea of new birth for the first time. For another it was a commitment to be born again. Someone else *felt* loved by God and was very thankful. For *me* it was a whole fresh look at the issues at stake in the dialog between Nicodemus and Jesus, and the implications of what Jesus was telling him.

The freshness came to me because God used the other members of the group. They asked questions and saw things I did not see because the territory was too familiar. The non-Christians taught me by their honest inquiry. The Word of God shouted new truth at me.

That's the reward of a small group Bible study that is controlled by the Holy Spirit. *He* really is the teacher. And he uses the experiences and insights of individual members to amplify truth. Studying in a group is a check on an individual's own understanding of the text. One person's commitment and honesty prods the reluctant heart of another.

Because it is so natural to speak of spiritual truth in small group studies, both Christian and non-Christian alike learn to verbalize about important matters of belief. For the Christian this is a sharpening of witness; for the non-Christian it brings into focus the issues at stake. Discussing can straighten out fuzzy thinking, especially when other group members join in the discussion. Becoming a Christian isn't an ABC plan which, when understood, takes care of the Christian life. It is establishing a relationship with the eternal God through Jesus Christ and making sense out of life. It is learning what the Lordship of Christ means in every part of life. This opportunity to verbalize, to sort out values and to grab hold of the importance and implications of what the Bible says stimulates growth on every level.

Some people act as though God is playing a game, trying to make us guess what he is saying to us—a kind of heavenly charade. In group Bible studies we hear God speak plainly and somehow know that it is he. We think about truth; it goes through our thought processes; we are encouraged by the perception of others; we have to react with truth.

Further, group Bible study teaches a pattern for personal Bible study, training members for a more thoughtful and disciplined investigation of truth. *There's more here than I know* becomes the humble attitude that keeps individuals from making hasty conclusions without adequate information. In short, it teaches a study pattern which affects the personal search for truth.

I've been speaking of small group studies in several contexts—a student study in a university dormitory and a women's study in a neighborhood. Let me add other kinds. One of the most rewarding of small group studies involves couples, because the husbands and wives learn and grow together and the implications of this for family life are so far-reaching. Couples studies may be in neighborhoods, in professions or in job contacts. Getting husbands and wives together for a regular weekly commitment is not the easiest thing you might try to do, but it will be rewarding.

Career friendships offer all sorts of possibilities—a bag lunch study for professors on a campus, an after-school study for school teachers, a noon hour study for engineers, secretaries, accountants. I know people who are involved in stimulating groups in each of these situations, and my own participation in these groups assures me that they are not only workable, but life-changing.

The tendency in beginning such a study is to

search out all the Christians available and gather them into the study. And while that may be worthy and conscience-salving, it doesn't meet the needs of the people around us who still don't know what they need to know about Jesus Christ. We need to say to our friends, "This book is changing my life. Come and study it with me!"

Small group studies change group life, too, in a different way. Some neighborhoods have been transformed. People who don't know each other come to share on deeper, meaningful levels of personhood. "Now I know why I was put on this street" has become a familiar comment.

I think of the first meeting of the Bible study in Lenore's neighborhood. One look around the room revealed women who were emotionally isolated from each other. One was a chic young woman who ran with her own sharp crowd; another was an older lady who seemed ill at ease and resentful; another was an immigrant from a strongly Catholic country. None of them knew each other well enough to share themselves on the simplest level.

By the time six weeks had passed, the neighborhood was knit together into a caring unit. The Catholic woman, who had wanted no part of what she thought would be a neighborhood religious war, found herself an enthusiastic member. The sullen older lady found out that God loved her, and that her neighbors did, too. They began to care for each others' children and property, as well as each other.

Frieda's mother was visiting her and they were at this particular neighborhood study together when the messenger from the United States government came to their house to deliver the word that their son and brother had been killed in Vietnam. A little boy, riding his bicycle on the front sidewalk, called to the messenger, "She's not home, Mister. All the mothers go to *that* house on Thursday morning."

Frieda later told me that had this news come three months earlier she would not have known anyone in town well enough to let them share in her sorrow. Now she was part of a loving group who ministered to her needs—some by bringing food and caring, others by praying and comforting, another by calling her minister—who became Frieda's minister.

This may not be a group's primary purpose; but it is a worthwhile by-product. One troubled woman commented to me, "Whenever I come to this Bible study, I feel loved."

Who should lead the discussion? Granted that we are committed to an inductive, discussion-type group study, there are two ways to handle leadership. One is to have a group leader, someone who takes responsibility for the group and prepares ahead of time for each study. This person uses discussion questions, but the leadership has the constancy of that person's particular style.

A second way, and a better one I think, is to rotate the leadership. That puts all group members on the same plane. If you use a good discussion guide, rotating the leadership works well. The person who leads the study always learns the most, so why not share that joy? Further, the one who leads the study knows how important good group participation is in making the study a profitable learning experience for everyone. This gives that person a different attitude towards being a participant and a responsible group member.

The advantage of rotation of leadership lies in what it does for individual members. We had decided to begin a study in a neighborhood in which I lived; the hour and day had been determined; all that was necessary was a volunteer to lead the first study. Dorothy said, "I'll do it." She studied the assigned Bible passage all week, and came to the group with an enthusiasm that was contagious. She said, "I've never gotten so much out of the Bible *in my life.* This discussion guide is such a help! I can hardly wait for you to share with me all that is in this chapter of Mark. You wouldn't believe all I learned this week!"

She had never led a group study like this one before. Her enthusiasm was not based on her own proven ability, but on the content of the passage. She did a good job in leading us into the truth of the portion we were studying. At the close of the time, she asked for a volunteer for next week. Lou was ready, saying, "That was so much fun, I want to try it."

Not all volunteers are equally gifted in leadership, but the strength and success of the study is dependent on the participation of the group more than on a strong leader. I believe this does more in the long run to encourage the spiritual growth of individual members by teaching them how to study the Bible than any other method. Again, the principle works best with a good study guide. (Making up good discussion questions which get at the meat of the passage is not as easy as most people think.) Going home with a glowy, emotional feeling because of the impact of a strong personality is not as important as feeling the powerful impact of the Holy Spirit's teaching. (However, the two are not necessarily mutually exclusive.)

The strength of the single leader plan is that this person usually reviews and summarizes with more force because he has a sense of continuity and responsibility for the whole. Knowing the big picture, this leader emphasizes and stresses important sections with more authority.

I am presently in studies with both of these leadership plans. In one I take my turn; in the second I lead the discussion each time. When I am forced to be absent, the second study flounders for a leader. In the first study, learning carries on as usual. Participation in the first group is consistently more reliable than in the second. Although members may feel they learn more in the second, I am inclined to feel that they do not become as familiar with the text as in the situation where each takes a turn.

Obviously God uses both. Each approach has advantages. A one-leader study does not have to become leader-centered. Often it does; but that is probably the result of the leader's technique in resorting to teaching, rather than leading a discussion. But a more serious problem is this: if we have to look for specially gifted leaders, we limit the number of studies we can have. When the group shares responsibility, the multiplication of Bible studies can have an exploding, first-century-church quality.

The idea is to foster group ownership of the study. Not Joe's Bible study, but *our* Bible study. Group ownership is essential to an on-going study. People have to own it to feel responsible for it and committed to it. That is why every effort should be made to avoid the idea of "Mrs. Johnson's study." The invitation is always to come to *our* study.

Keep the group small. In our success culture, we often feel if we have twenty people present we have twice as good a study as when we have ten present. When a group gets to be larger than eight or ten, it's time to think and pray about splitting up into two or more small groups. This idea may not find favor with people who have grown to enjoy being together, and it does have to be done lovingly with the Holy Spirit's help.

Why form two groups out of one? Because the goal is one hundred percent participation. When the study becomes too large, some people are afraid to share, to expose themselves. Others don't feel responsible to do so. Let someone else talk. The small group is more supportive to its members and seems to learn more than the unwieldly ones; It stands to reason that it is easier to get to know eight people well than it is fifteen. And a group of five or six will have a deeper time of sharing.

In our town two Christians live side by side. Each felt a neighborhood Bible study was a good idea. After discussing it together, they decided that each of them would begin a study and invite people from their end of the block. Women from the far end were pleased to hear that friends down the street were also attending a study. Now members of the two study groups check on each other to see who is studying what. The block has never had so many good and important conversations. It must be a great street to live on!

Start small

Mention a small group Bible study to some people and they picture a safe, sanctimonious, conservative and very uptight circle of people who use spiritual clichès and who know all the answers. I can never be quite sure why that mental image appears. Is it because we want an excuse to not participate—or do we hope it will be like that because it would be safer and more predictable?

The real picture focuses in on a conglomerate group—women in jeans and hair rollers (they interrupted their ironing to come to the study), doubting men being driven by the Holy Spirit to belief in the text, or people smoking up a storm as the ideas become increasingly exciting. A Jewish woman, basically non-religious, yet conscious of Jewishness and struggling over the Messiah-idea is there. A thorough-going humanist is being exposed to supernatural concepts. Another person may be a non-reader, unfamiliar with discussing ideas. An incipient alcoholic struggles with discomfort in the presence of seemingly religious, disciplined group members. In short, small group studies are the stuff out of which life is made.

Is it safe? As safe as life with Jesus Christ always is. He sometimes takes us on great adventures and into water over our heads, but he is always there. The idea of changing people through personal encounter with God is his idea. We can expect him to be present each time we gather.

Mark wrote of such an encounter in his Gospel.

As he (Jesus) walked along he saw a tax collector, Levi, the son of Alphaeus, sitting in his office. Jesus said to him, "Follow me." Levi got up and followed him.

Later on Jesus was having a meal in Levi's house. There were many tax collectors and outcasts who were following Jesus, and some of them joined him and his disciples at the table. Some teachers of the Law who were Pharisees, saw that Jesus was eating with these outcasts and tax collectors; so they asked the disciples, "Why does he eat with tax collectors and outcasts?" Jesus heard them and answered: "People who are well do not need a doctor, but only those who are sick. I have not come to call the respectable people, but the outcasts." Mark 2:14-17 (Today's English Version)

Look back over this story and do your own inductive study, using the following discussion questions:

What kind of a person was Levi when Jesus called him? (What was his profession? For whom did he collect taxes? What might his reputation in the community have been because of his association with the Roman government?)

Why did Jesus call Levi?

Would you have thought him a likely candidate for discipleship? Why?

Why do we see so few Levis contacted today?

What did Levi do after his decision to follow Jesus?

What was the Pharisees' reaction to Jesus' presence at Levi's dinner?

Put Jesus' response in your own words.

What do you learn from this incident about a) your judgment of people's interest? b) your involvement in the world? c) the message you have to share?

Applying this passage we see several truths. First, we often pre-judge whom the Lord will call. We look at people from the outside and draw decisive conclusions about who is interested in knowing God (and who God is interested in knowing). Secure looking people who seem to have everything probably wouldn't be interested, we think. Or we look at their nationality or religious heritage and cancel that person out. If they are coarse and uncultured we are sure they would be offensive to God. How differently Jesus looked at people!

When I was a sophomore in college I got my first lesson in this, written in big Dick and Jane letters so I couldn't miss the point. A wealthy girl lived in a large room at the end of our hall. She had several extra wardrobe closets in her room, full of clothes designed and made for her. A beautiful, chic girl any day of the week, when she went out on a date she was simply "smashing." We used to feign reasons to be out in the hall to see what new creation she was wearing. She frequently dated the son of a boomingly successful industrialist. He was known to throw pebbles at her window and when she opened, he tossed a box of orchids into her hands. Neat, eh?

It never once occurred to me that this wonder-girl should be invited to the Bible study we had on our floor. I never suspected she knew what *need* was—until one night when she knocked on my door, came in and opened up her empty heart. As I said before, God got the point across to me rather clearly. You *can't* tell from the outside who is a likely candidate for the kingdom of God. So we spread the net wide and invite everyone we can to come and see who Jesus is.

Second, the message is a *Person*. It is not our church or our own life-style. We want people to have an encounter with Jesus Christ, not adopt our

Sunday behavior patterns—or anything which may be merely cultural.

Third, we need to learn to be at home with all kinds of people. The unique thing about God's family, the church, is that the candidate must acknowledge that he is unworthy for membership before he gets in. Try joining any other society by confessing that you are a sinner and a failure! That is precisely what Jesus is saying when he tells the Pharisees that people who think they are well never call for a doctor.

I remember telling a co-worker about the husband of a woman in our Bible study. The grace and goodness of God had reached into this lovely woman's life and she was very dear to him and to us. I was almost outraged at the miserable, irrational, illogical, ill-tempered (you fill in the rest) husband she had to live with every day. I had seen her hurt so often and, though I prayed for him, I had already written "no hope" over his head. My friend listened to my hot description of this pathetic man, smiled and said confidently, "That's just the kind of person God loves to redeem."

You already know what happened. Those words of my friend were prophetic!

Perhaps by now you are ready to ask, *How do I start such a Bible study*? There are several ways.

First, pray for a meaningful conversation with one other person in your sphere of contacts that could lead into either a) actually reading the Bible together or b) suggesting a group Bible study. Sometimes a study branches out from two of you meeting regularly to discuss the Bible together. The biggest step in beginning is *the decision to do it*; God seems to take our confidence in him seriously and provides opportunities beyond our courage.

One of my friends, a new believer who has good rapport in the neighborhood, simply called up a number of neighbors and said, "Hey, I'm really in on something new and want to learn more about it. I just discovered the Bible and wonder if several of us could get together and study it." She invited them for coffee at a specific time to plan the group, showed them the study guide—and a small group Bible study was on its way. Did anyone refuse to participate? Only one who admitted the idea scared her. But, interestingly, after almost every study the scared friend inquires into the group's discussion.

Another method developed by *Neighborhood Bible Studies, Inc.* (see Chapter 7 for the story of this organization) has repeatedly proven both appealing and workable. The strength of this approach is that it enables the person beginning the study to participate as a peer group member in the study, eliminating the tendency of the group to believe that the person beginning the study must also be the answer man. This is particularly important in neighborhood studies.

Lila Jones decides God wants her to begin a neighborhood study. Perhaps by now she already knows of one other interested person in the neighborhood who supports this idea. On the other hand, she may hardly know any of her neighbors. She gives a neighborhood coffee, extending the invitation to *every* house as far down the block as she wishes to go, and across the street. (In other words, she doesn't pre-judge who will be interested.) The invitation is to a coffee and to meet a friend who will share some ideas about a neighborhood discussion group, using the Bible as a study book.

At one house the woman says, "I'm interested in the coffee, but not in the Bible."

"Fine," says Lila. "There's no obligation at all. Come for coffee just to be with the rest of the neighbors."

If Lila is like most of us she may have some shaky moments over this new project of hers. It does take courage. But she prays and believes it is God's idea. She invites fourteen women. Twelve show up on Tuesday morning at 9:45.

The group spends half an hour chatting together, then Lila introduces a friend from outside the neighborhood who explains the idea. The friend talks about the advantage of having a regular opportunity to be together and come to know each other really well, while at the same time learning something important. She mentions other groups across the country who are doing this and finding the Bible a rewarding book to study. No one teaches the group, she says, but the members read the chapters and with the use of good discussion questions they dig into the text and discover what it is saying. It is not for experts, but for people who want to learn. Group members take turns leading the study, using a prepared guide. The variety of their backgrounds enriches the study and provides a stimulus for learning.

She suggests that they do a brief study together to illustrate what she is talking about. She has asked Lila to have a Bible ready for everyone, with a marker at the page they will study. She leads a brief study, using discussion questions, urging everyone to investigate the passage, trying to get everyone present to participate in the discussion.

When she has finished answering any questions the women have about the concept of a small group Bible study, and has shown them the guide, she turns the group's response back to Lila. Lila may ask, "What do you think? Would any of you be interested?" From that point on all that must be decided is the day, the time, and the place. Then, "Who wants to lead the first study?"

Does it work? Yes. Someone always responds at the end of the presentation. It may be, "This is just what I need," or, "I'd like to try it. I don't know very much about the Bible, but I'd like to learn." God always works in someone ahead of time, and others join in the same response.

It's the risk of faith. Lila and her friend trusted God in this venture. Later Lila helps her friend in *her* neighborhood by being the outsider who explains the idea.

We began to put his idea into practice in our own sophisticated town several years ago. I was the friend from outside the neighborhood who began explaining the idea. Then women who had already begun Bible studies began helping others start studies. The idea has mushroomed so that at the end of four years I knew of thirty neighborhood Bible studies in the city of Ann Arbor, plus many in outlying communities. Today I have lost all track of how many studies exist because their development has been so spontaneous. Only recently I met a woman at a club meeting, and in the course of conversation she mentioned a Bible study group she attended in her neighborhood—a new one I hadn't heard about—explaining it to me with enthusiasm because she didn't know if I had ever heard of the idea.

In some neighborhoods where we have used this idea, the person beginning the study had never met some of her neighbors. She called names, but had no faces to go with them in her mind. But the women came, and as they walked in the door they introduced themselves to her—and to me, the guest in the neighborhood. They were delighted that someone had at last come up with a way to get acquainted.

Obviously, this is not the only way to begin a study. I have already mentioned less structured ways. But it is an idea that works, and I have gone into detail about it because it provides the boost many need to get started.*

Clearly this method enhances the initiator's ability to operate as a peer group member and fosters group ownership of the study.

In another neighborhood where people live isolated from each other in large homes on acre lots, a woman sent out invitations to a coffee and an opportunity to hear about Jesus Christ. (She put that right on the invitation.) Twenty neighbors came. It was a coffee, a get acquainted time, and a forthright presentation of the Gospel. Several women became Christians as a result—and three study groups are now being held in that neighborhood.

It's not just for neighborhoods. These are simply workable ideas and good illustrations. Adapt them. Expand them. Be flexible. Some idea will surely fit your situation.

A most important tool for the small group study is an adequate guide. This means that someone ahead of you has studied the passage in-

*Details for sample study are found in *How to Start a Neighborhood Bible Study,* published by *Neighborhood Bible Studies, Inc.,* Box 222, Dobbs Ferry, N. Y. 10522.

tensely, has discovered some of the gems, the truths, the relationships, the applications. They have formed their discoveries into questions to help the group dig out the content for themselves. Good questions drive the group into the text to find answers, and are worded in such a way that a superficial answer is not enough. A good guide insists that you get the facts before you make any attempt to interpret or apply what you've read.

Guides designed for small group studies are available from:

Harold Shaw Publishers, Box 567, Wheaton, Ill. 60187

Neighborhood Bible Studies, Inc., Box 222, Dobbs Ferry, New York 10522

Tyndale House Publishers, 336 Gundersen Drive, Wheaton, Ill. 60187

Inter-Varsity Press, Box F, Downers Grove, Ill. 60515

Most studies are from New Testament books, although a few are on Old Testament books or characters. Many experienced leaders suggest that groups begin studying with the Gospel of Mark. It is the shortest of the Gospels, full of brief vignettes that reveal Jesus as a person, and contains lots of action. By all means have a study on hand to recommend, since a diverse group will usually choose a difficult book like the *Revelation* (always expect that as a suggestion!) rather than a Gospel which would introduce them to Jesus Christ.

In most studies we encourage a variety of translations. Some people haven't discovered that God doesn't need to speak 17th century English. They have kept him at a distance because they assume they cannot understand what he is saying. Modern translations such as *Phillips'* and *Living Letters* are particularly useful for those who are unfamiliar with the Bible. The variety of translations may be confusing to some in the group until they get used to it. They will say, "My Bible doesn't say that," until someone explains that all our versions are different translations from the same Greek manuscripts, and basically all translations say the same thing. The advantage of all having the same edition is that group members can turn to the same page number, which saves embarrassment in finding the way through the Bible. The advantage of a variety of translations is the additional light thrown on the passage by the different word choices.

I personally have reservations about the use of Bibles with notes. They can kill discussion; but worse, they more often make it unnecessary to think. The notes are not inspired; the biblical text is. Why let the notes cheat us out of honest investigation? One Bible study was almost driven into the ground by a woman reading notes from the Interpreter's Bible, which to her bore the same weight as the biblical text. The same danger is inherent in a Bible with Scofield's notes. Some of these notes are indeed enlightening—as is any reference book, but they need to be used with care.

In one study I remember a question designed to get group members to investigate the real meaning of biblical belief by asking for synonyms for *believe*. Someone had an *Amplified New Testament* and before the others could think, he read off the list of synonyms which are part of the text of that Bible. That finished that. It isn't hearing a list read that helps individuals; it is *thinking* and coming to conclusions that help us.

On the other hand, in a study on the book of Romans, group members struggled to grasp the concept of what it meant to be dead to sin, but alive to God in Christ. One person finally said, "Oh, look. This shows what it means!" She displayed the simple line drawings from *Good News for Modern Man*—a bent figure carrying a heavy load, laying the load at the foot of the cross, and walking away beyond the cross, erect and upright.

God will be pleased to use many surprising ways to teach members of studies like the ones I've just described. No wonder people say, "Wednesday is the best day of the week for me. It's the day our Bible study meets."

Don't tell!
Ask!

Every neighborhood is different. So is every employment grouping or any other place we might try to make this idea work. So far, I haven't discovered a typical *anywhere* that guarantees a certain number of people with Type A, B or C personalities. That's probably just as well because then we would set up a model and convince ourselves that since our situation wasn't model an idea like small group studies would never work for us! The variety is part of the humor and wonder of the situation.

When Shirley described the people in her neighborhood to me, I could see why she had reservations about the kind of response we would get in presenting the idea of a Bible study. Four were completely unchurched, their knowledge of any biblical facts rated zero. One of these four was a grandmother, excessively quiet, with almost a psychopathic silence about her. Another was new in the community, completely without friends or interests, and having made her house into an attractive home, she was often seen sitting in a chair, looking out the window—by the hour. A frozen kind of a person, as if she had been hurt too many times to want to feel any more. The other two were bouncy and pagan.

In addition to Shirley, the group netted three others. One was a warm-hearted person who had prayed with Shirley about beginning the group. The other two were believers, but the kind who feel called to be special guardians of truth and to demonstrate all they know about the Bible in every conversation.

I was there to introduce the study. We did a sample study suggested by *Neighborhood Bible Studies* from Mark 2:1-12 to demonstrate the possibilities of such a study. I wanted to get everyone to talk during the discussion because a contribution in conversation indicates that people are opening up to the idea of participating. The story was about the paralytic let down through the roof, and the point of the study, as facts would reveal, was Jesus' declaration of his power to forgive sins by making the paralytic walk—an outright claim to deity.

I asked the group to set the scene, to describe

what they saw in their minds from the account we had read. I asked why and how Jesus' preaching was interrupted. I kept trying to draw out the quiet ones and the ones scared of the Bible, and they were responding. My problem was the Christian vigilantes who wanted to get to the point quickly and preach the Gospel. At every point they wanted to force the text to say more than it said; they wanted to rush on to the implications of Jesus' claim to deity; they flipped back and forth to other references; they tried desperately to preach their sermon. They didn't trust the Holy Spirit to use the text of the passage to convince those present. In short, they were completely insensitive to the insecurities of the others.

But they were insecure, too. They had never been in a situation like this before. They had either been preached to or done the preaching. The concept of examining the evidence was new to them, and they were afraid that the truth might be missed, so they forced it.

Who but the Holy Spirit can handle one like this? Surprisingly, a group did begin in that neighborhood, greased by the oil of the Holy Spirit. The non-Christians stayed and eventually the most verbal of the vigilantes told Shirley that she didn't enjoy that kind of a group because it didn't come to the point fast enough for her. She left and joined a church group where everyone had her cultural background. I'm sorry, in a way, that she left. She *needed* the group, if just to deepen her own sensitivity. But more than that, she needed to see how great God is, how he uses his Word to change us and how powerful truth really is.

I have been in other studies where some person delighted in being controversial or took pleasure in misunderstanding. Everyone's teeth were set on edge by such an abrasive personality. What did we do? Prayed. God either changed or removed the person so that others could progress in learning and group relationships.

Which brings us to the problem of handling the dynamics of a group. Create an atmosphere in which everyone who comes feels free to be who he really is. That is one reason the groups should be kept small. The situation is not threatening: you don't have to know a given amount of information to participate. The goal is one hundred percent participation and people should feel free to disagree, to admit to confusion and lack of understanding, and to bring up related questions and not be made to feel stupid.

Arranging the seating wisely helps group interaction. If the group fits around a table, that arrangement provides a sense of closeness, informality and a place to put your coffee cup. (Serving a cup of coffee and a cookie or the equivalent relaxes people and fosters a sense of belonging.) Wherever you sit—whether in the living room or in the kitchen or dining room or some club room—

make sure each person can see all the others in the group. And, of course, everyone should have their own copy of the Bible.

If there are smokers in the group, ashtrays should be conveniently placed. Often people will smoke with increasing fury with the stimulus of ideas, so make sure the room has adequate ventilation. And not just ventilation for smoke, but sufficient fresh air to keep people alert to participate (especially if the group meets after lunch.)

What do you do when you throw out a question for discussion and the person who answers it completely misses the point? Or maybe only part of the question is answered?

Wait for more discussion. Have a positive attitude to all contributions. Never say, as the leader, "That's wrong," or "That's a good answer" in a way that evaluates the worth of a person's contribution. If the answer is inadequate, ask, "What do some of the rest of you think?" or "What other observations can you make?" and look around at other group members.

If the answer is clearly off-track, ask, "What verse are you referring to?" or "Where do you find that in the passage?" Our goal is to make people feel comfortable while at the same time handling the text with integrity. If someone waxes eloquent on their own opinions, one of the above questions can be asked to reaffirm that we stick to the text we are studying.

When the discussion indicates that the passage has been misunderstood, ask someone to read it again, preferably the person who mis-read it.

In keeping with the rule of making everyone feel at ease, don't ask anyone to read aloud unless you know for sure that they like to read. Ask for volunteers instead. I've known of people who have avoided group Bible study for fear they would be asked to either read aloud or pray. I put that in the ground rules of the study: reading aloud is on a volunteer basis; and no one will be asked to pray unless first consulted.

Encourage people to use the index if they aren't familiar enough with the Bible to find their way around in it. That's what it is there for; make it a natural thing to use it.

The leader must be careful not to talk too much. The traffic pattern of group contribution should not be from leader to group member and then back to leader. Allow time for group discussion. If you wait, others will share their thoughts, particularly on interpretation and application questions. When the leader rushes from question to question, keeping a tight rein on discussion, the group tends to become rigid and mechanical.

The leader can encourage less talkative members by eye-contact, by waiting a sufficient amount of time, or by asking an opinion question in a sensitive way. The too-talkative can be quieted by your eye-contact with the non-talkers. If some-

this

not this

DIAGRAM OF GROUP INTERACTION

one is always quick to give an answer, reassure the group by asking, "What do the rest of you think?"

Periods of silence don't always have to be filled immediately. Allow members time to digest what they are discovering. If a silence means the question isn't clear, re-state the question.

A group feeling and loyalty will grow after a few meetings. People will build the group into their schedule, begin to feel increasingly safe with others, and a warm sense of fellowship will develop.

Basic ground rules for operation should be given when the group begins, repeated when new members join, and reviewed when the group moves into new study material.

Ground rules for good studies:

1) Stick to the chapter under discussion. Don't cross-reference all over the Bible unless the study guide calls for you to look up pertinent references. (The quickest way to make the novice feel inept is to have some group member say, "This reminds me of a passage in Jeremiah . . ," especially when the novice doesn't even know Jeremiah is part of the Bible.) Build a frame of reference for the group in the book you are studying, so that as the study continues members may refer back to portions they have studied together.

2) Decide together to avoid tangents because of your commitment to find out what the passage being studied says. Help one another keep this rule. Leaders should learn to say, "Well, back to the text . . . " or "The next question is . . . " If the tangent is crucial, take time for it immediately. There will always be some exceptions. But most tangents can be postponed by simply suggesting that they be discussed after today's study is over.

3) Commit yourself to participate. The group is enlivened by a sense of responsibility to participate on the part of each group member.

4) Start and stop on time. This is a vital rule, especially in women's groups. If the study is set from 10 to 11:15 and regularly runs overtime to 11:45, some will begin to drop out because they can't afford that much time. Keep your word. If it is to begin at 10 a.m., begin at 10 a.m.

5) Allow the chapter to speak for itself. Don't force it to say more than it does; don't feel you have to strengthen it. Discover what the author is saying. Let the document be the authority.

6) Use modern translations, or at least have them available in the study. *The Revised Standard Version, Good News for Modern Man, Williams', The Living Bible, Phillips'* and the *New English Bible* are some of the most popular versions.

7) Come as you are. Especially if this is a neighborhood day-time study. If you can come as you are, you can return home to the interrupted task more easily.

8) No one will be asked to read or pray aloud without being consulted first.

9) Keep a good dictionary on hand to help you look up words you don't understand. A good map is also a handy study tool.

10) Don't bring commentaries to the study. Use them at home to help you understand, but leave them there. If more help is needed than you can get from the text, the study guide should provide it. Commentaries are helpful, but they also make people mentally lazy.

11) Learn to handle difficulties wisely. "When you come to a problem in Bible study, treat it as you would a bone while eating a fish. Take the bone out and carry on with the fish. After you have finished the fish, come back and collect the bones." (Dr. Oswald Smith.)

12) Keep the goal of the study group in mind.

The Leader's Responsibility

The leader's responsibility is to prepare ahead of time, so that the time allotted can be maximized. As you study the passage, it will be obvious that some passages deserve more emphasis than others. The leader is aware of the amount of material to be covered and should move the study along so that time doesn't run out, keeping the study on target.

The leader should start and stop the study according to the agreed time.

The leader should encourage members to share in personal application of what has been learned.

Since everyone will be both leader and participant in studies where the leadership is rotated on a volunteer basis, members of the group can help each other to practice the group dynamics discussed in this chapter.

I have personally found it exciting to see the way group study sharpens personal observation. People begin to see how paragraphs relate to each other; they notice the specific choice of certain words, the impact of the verbs used. Contrasts, connectives, repetitions are picked up. Observations are made about relationships within the Godhead. When individual members begin to practice these basics of observation their own personal Bible study is bound to be enhanced. They are developing patterns of study in a group context.

A Word to the Wise
In a diverse group there will undoubtedly be some Christians who have had the advantage of good Bible teaching and who see the big picture in a way that most of the group does not. Here are some hints to help your participation to be a blessing rather than a frustration to others.

1) Let the Holy Spirit be the teacher. Don't preach.

2) Don't over-spiritualize or over-apply. Never say more than the Bible says!

3) Don't let what you know scare others away. Don't pontificate. If asked a question, turn it into a question for the group.

4) Don't feel responsible to correct every heretical idea that hits the airwaves in the course of discussion. Most of them are irrelevant and die a natural death without your help.

5) Look for fresh ways to see and say old truths. Avoid clichés.

6) Expect God to teach you more than you've ever learned before.

I have mentioned the importance of *letting the document be the authority*. Quietly following that principle will eliminate tense moments.

John, a brand new believer in a dormitory on the campus of the University of Illinois, wanted to start a Bible study in his dorm. He asked my husband to help him prepare the study, to pray with him and to be on hand to bail him out if a distress signal came.

He had chosen to do *John's Gospel* and entered boldly into a discussion of the first eighteen verses of the chapter with the ten fellows who showed up for the study. One of the ten was conversant with the Greek concept of *logos,* translated *word* in John, chapter one. He began to elaborate on the *logos* concept and Greek thought, getting the study off-track and raising arguments about the use of the word in this chapter.

My husband waited for the distress signal, feeling John was probably in over his head. But it never came. Though John was a novice, he knew the text was the authority, and the Holy Spirit put it in his mind to say, "That's interesting, Tom, but who do you fellows think John, the writer of this book, had in mind when he wrote about the Word?" And they were back on track.

In one neighborhood where I was introducing the idea of a small group study, a professor's wife commented, "I don't know if I believe the Bible is true or not. That's why I question the value of my attending a study like this."

I, too, got help from Outside and heard myself saying, "You don't have to decide now whether the Bible is true. We simply invite you to read and discuss what Mark, a follower of Jesus Christ, believed and wrote about Jesus. In a way, don't you think your own intellectual integrity demands that you investigate and decide for yourself?" She agreed.

We don't have to argue, to feel afraid, or protect Truth. After all, who needs to defend a Lion?

The fruit
of a
good idea

The combination of a good idea, the right timing and perserverance has produced an expansive organization you ought to know about: *Neighborhood Bible Studies, Inc.*

As organizations go, it's not exactly the Organization Man, since it consists of the two women who came up with the idea and the perserverance. Plus a Board of Directors and a secretary. The expansive part of the organization? The hundreds of people involved in small group studies who may not even realize that they are part of *Neighborhood Bible Studies, Inc.* But Kay Schell and Marilyn Kunz never had in mind building a dynasty; they only wanted to share a workable idea and see people introduced to Jesus Christ.

Marilyn Kunz used to dream that when she

grew up she'd marry a millionaire, have dozens of cats, sit on a flowered chaise lounge in a sunny bedroom and eat fresh boxes of chocolates every day while reading children's books.

Kay Schell was going to be a nurse, a modern Florence Nightingale, wear a white uniform, a starchy cap and make everyone who was sick well again and everyone who was sad happy.

Today they are associate directors of *Neighborhood Bible Studies,* a movement only slightly related to chocolates and making the sick well. Unless, of course, you think of spiritual chocolates and spiritual health. How their movement came into existence is part of the exciting story of what God has been doing in small group studies across the country.

Marilyn became a Christian in her freshman year of high school through a history teacher, who was also a riding instructor. Imagine a Christian who could ride horses like that, Marilyn thought. And she listened to what this teacher said and became a believer.

She later went to Wheaton College, where she majored in English literature, then on to Biblical Seminary in New York where she was given large doses of inductive Bible study training. She taught Bible in the public schools of Virginia, and later became a Director of Religious Education in a church. In 1957 she joined the staff of Inter-Varsity Christian Fellowship (IVCF), itinerating to various college campuses in the New England area, sparking dorm Bible studies wherever she could.

Meanwhile Kay Schell had entered nursing at Columbia University-Presbyterian Hospital in New York City and became that white-uniformed nurse she had dreamed about. In training for nursing, she became acquainted with the Nurses Christian Fellowship, a branch of IVCF. Having grown up in a biblically-oriented church, she was equipped and eager to be part of the NCF witnessing fellowship.

Her commitment and her ability to influence others in areas of godliness led Joseph Bayly, then with IVCF, to encourage her to join the staff of the Nurses Christian Fellowship. For ten years she visited schools of nursing in New England, New York City, and the Hudson River Valley. A major part of her ministry involved influencing nursing students to dare to begin small group Bible studies as a way to expose their fellow-students to truth about Jesus Christ.

In 1960 both Marilyn and Kay had battle fatigue from their forays onto the campuses in their areas. Marilyn started dreaming about that millionaire again and Kay thought of returning to nursing. Instead God gave them a great idea.

They had seen God use inductive Bible studies in small groups on the campus. Why wouldn't it work in neighborhoods?

One woman in Waterville, Maine had opened her home at their encouragement and invited her neighbors in. It was a brand new idea to most of them, but it worked. Sitting around the room investigating what the Bible said was more exciting than they imagined. Their enthusiasm spread to others, and Kay and Marilyn were on hand to capitalize on the idea.

Neighborhood Bible studies began providing a warm spot in the spiritually cold East. People were eager—more hungry than they knew. Neighborhood groups brought about a cross-pollinization between churches; Christians began reaching out to others. From numerous sources they received names of people who might be interested. By this time they had resigned from Inter-Varsity staff and were giving all their time to establishing neighborhood groups.

They had begun in the Fall and by January of the first year they had twelve active Bible studies in key locations in the northern and western suburbs of New York City—not an easy place to break ground. By June twenty studies were meeting, and they were busy preparing study guides for the groups to use. Six years later (1966) they incorporated as a non-profit faith organization.

A good idea sends its seeds to places never known before, and Kay and Marilyn have long since lost track of the exact numbers of neighborhood Bible studies. Their best clue comes from the hundred and hundreds of study guides that are ordered, but even then it is difficult to know the impact of a concept that has spread across the country.

People share the idea with their friends. A new study begins. Someone moves and a whole series of studies begin in a new city. Pressure on ministers to be more biblical in their sermons comes from women who have found Life in neighborhood Bible studies.

Each Spring Kay and Marilyn make a tour from the East through the Midwest, holding Bible study seminars in key cities. In some places they hold twenty-four hour retreats which provide opportunity for a deeper teaching ministry.

Their method is the inductive study of the Scriptures; their technique is the same one described in this book. Neighborhood Bible studies all across the country, as well as other small group studies in churches and among professional people, are indebted to Marilyn and Kay for the study guides they have been writing, testing and publishing.

Kay and Marilyn work more closely with the numerous studies near them in Westchester County, New York, branching out to hold frequent workshops in New Jersey, Connecticut and Pennsylvania where there has been multiplication of the idea. Writing and refining the guides is a major part of their work schedule, undergirded by their earnest prayers that many will come to spiritual life because of Neighborhood Bible Studies.

Study guides are crucial to good studies. The questions must get at the facts, provoke thought and stimulate investigation and application. They must not be so simple that they insult the intelligence of the group nor so profound that members are scared off. Back-up questions keep the superficial answers in check. This is not a fill-in-the-blank approach.

Kay and Marilyn urge groups to begin with *Mark's Gospel* and then proceed to *Acts, John* and *Romans.* Some members want to push ahead to harder studies in *Romans* and *Hebrews* before the rest of their group is ready. The person who initiates the study has a leadership responsibility to consider very carefully the material to be studied. Each group varies in its background. Various parts of the country have a different climate of religious knowledge. Enough studies are now available so that you can have an appropriate one for your group.

I'm partial to *John's Gospel* and have prepared a study on the whole book called *Eyewitness: John's View of Jesus.* This can be used as a beginning study, whereas a further guide on the Sermon on the Mount* requires a more mature group and some experience in studying together.

Kay and Marilyn held Neighborhood Bible

The God Who Understands Me, Harold Shaw Publishers, 1971.

Studies workshops in the Philadelphia area where Martha Reapsome was an enthusiastic initiator of studies. Martha later moved to Ohio and met Sue Burnham, whose husband pastors The Chapel on Fir Hill in Akron. And thereby hangs a tale.

Sue Burnham caught Martha's enthusiasm for small group study and used the discussion idea in a mental hospital where she was working. The response was surprising and rewarding. She shared the concept with women in their church and invited interested members to a workshop session to get hold of the idea. They contacted the church membership, forming eight studies in various parts of the city. To the Burnhams' delight, they found the women ready and willing for such an adventure. They brought their friends; the groups grew and divided.

At Christmas time they held holiday coffees in homes, urging members to bring their friends to hear the Christmas message. Over 500 attended and again they announced the presence of the small group studies scattered over the city and invited interested visitors to join them.

In a year and a half the groups multiplied to thirty-six. Three studies spun off from one study. The studies are connected with the church only in that the groups have been initiated by church members, though encouragement and training also comes from the church.

Pastor David Burnham refers new converts in

his church to the Bible studies nearest their own neighborhood because these small groups provide the care and teaching so important for new believers. "The members of these Bible studies," said Mr. Burnham, "are the most eager participants in the worship services of the church. Their faces show their enthusiasm for the Word of God, and they need less pastoral care than any others in the church. So many spiritual needs are being met in the small groups."

David Burnham is enthusiastic about the inductive small group outreach. He sees the members of the church growing and reaching out to their friends and neighbors. Obviously, he cannot control this movement and there are already more studies than he knows about, but this fact does not intimidate him. He considers it a healthy mark of a New Testament church.

Every other Saturday morning the men gather at the church and bring *their* friends. They have a breakfast snack together and break up into study groups of eight, again using discussion questions. About fifty participate in these Saturday morning studies for men.

The Burnhams—and the members of The Chapel on Fir Hill—are excited about this approach to Bible study. They now know of about fifty studies, including the men's studies, which are related to the church, and many more have grown out of these. When Kay and Marilyn came to hold their first Bible Study Workshop on a blizzardy winter day, one hundred fifty women from all over Akron attended.

The study still goes on in the mental hospital. Elsewhere in Akron twenty senior citizens meet in a residence for Bible study. The college group and the young career girls in the church have grabbed hold of the idea and their groups are growing.

Sue's sisters had been teaching Bible studies in South Bend, Indiana, and when Sue told them about this new idea, they were reluctant to switch to so revolutionary a concept as group leadership. But they tried it. South Bend now has twenty studies functioning there and, as Sue's sister remarked, that easily triples the number of people they were reaching with a teacher-taught lesson. And it has not finished growing.

As I said, spread a good idea around with the guidance of our Heavenly Father and the power of the Holy Spirit and be prepared for an explosion of new Life.

**It
will cost
you**

Sonya came across the room after the study and
sat next to me on the sofa. "Something is happening to me," she said, "and I don't know what it is.
I seem to be different inside; even my husband has
noticed. All of the ways I used to react—fretting,
worrying, losing my temper—I don't act that way
so much anymore."

She had a look of wonder on her face as she
spoke. And what she was describing to me as she
continued was so obviously the work of God's
Spirit in her that I said, "It's almost as though you
had become a new person, isn't it? Like being born
a second time."

"Yes, yes," she said in her Swedish way.
"That's exactly how it feels."

God wants people to know when they are part

of his family so they can fully enjoy his fellowship and participate in the privileges of family life. Sonya needed to hear again exactly how one becomes a Christian, to know for sure that she had come to Christ and that he had made her righteous in God's sight through her personal faith.

Imagine being a member of the King's family and not knowing it! Very often people are born into the Christian family in small group studies, but are almost unaware of what is happening to them. They come week by week and simply believe. No great thunderclap, just believing and obeying.

Someone needs to help them understand. And that someone is probably you. Involving yourself in a small group study is always more than merely showing up at the appointed time. It means caring for the people who come. This will find you stopping by for coffee with someone or arranging for extra time with another. It will mean many telephone calls and conversations. Getting in on what God wants to do in the world costs something. It will cost *you*.

God has pushed me out into my community many times, and I look back on some of these events with awe. He *allowed* me to be part of many miracles.

One day during the study I noticed Barbara's eyes filled with tears. Afterwards I stood next to her and heard myself ask, "May I come over for a cup of coffee this afternoon?" Her response was a grateful, "Would you, please?"

She got right to the point almost the minute I walked in the door. She didn't know for sure if she was a Christian. She traced her past experiences for me, but she was filled with doubt about her present realities. We sat at her round oak kitchen table and I told her the story of a farmer who kept doubting whether he had experienced "new birth" in Christ. Over and over he gave himself to God, but later in the press of life, he was subject to terrible doubts. One day he went in the field, drove a stake in the ground, and again called on the name of the Lord to be saved, claiming God's promise that whoever comes to him will not be cast out. Later when he was tempted to doubt, he returned to the stake and reassured himself that he was in God's family. All he needed to do was claim the family privileges of daily cleansing through Jesus Christ.

That day Barbara made her oak kitchen table her "stake" and gave her heart to Christ. What did it matter if she thought she might have done it before? We didn't need to figure out the past; we needed to make sure of the present and the future.

She wasn't used to praying aloud, so I suggested we pray back and forth between us—brief prayers because God was in the room and we could both talk with him. I recount this prayer time because as we were praying, Barbara was obviously still keeping God at arm's length. Her confession of sin was like a community speech. I felt led to pray, "Oh, God, please help Barbara to really open up to you. You already know all about her. Please help her to be honest." The floodgate broke. Barbara came out into the open and stopped hiding from God.

Not having to hide meant being free to enjoy a relationship with God. In the days that followed Barbara's biblical intake quadrupled. And because God is such a good teacher, such a faithful Father, he began putting his divine finger on first one area of her life that needed some straightening and then another. Often it was painful, but she was learning how to deal with sin. It hurt to look someone up and apologize for lies; it was even more painful to send a check to pay for something stolen. But always there was the cleansing, healing and refreshing that made life sweeter afterwards.

Being involved with Barbara taught me far more than I can ever share.

Some people are plagued with terrible feelings of worthlessness and have trouble really believing God can accept them as they are. They keep trying to be good enough to be Christians—even when they hear Jesus saying so clearly that eternal life is not to be earned but is a gift of his grace. Trying to be good enough must be life's most frustrating experience. Freedom comes only when we accept his forgiveness and the new life he gives. Wherever we can lovingly re-emphasize this good news we need to do it.

Marian was that kind of woman. Her personal life was messy and as a result she was defensive and easily offended. She had been an off-and-on member of the group Bible study for about four years. Mostly off. The fifth year she brought a neighbor and came with disciplined regularity.

As time progressed she looked less sullen, became more friendly and open. Her participation in the study made me believe that something new was beginning inside her. But how could I ask her what it was without offending her? I decided to wait.

One day she called to tell me that their television had broken down and she was so happy. Somehow I had the good sense not to inquire into the relationship of a broken TV and happiness until she told me. A broken TV meant there was nothing to sit and look at after a hard day's work, so she and her husband had actually talked together. They had a wonderful conversation, she said. About God. And she was able to tell him all about the things she had been learning in Bible study.

Finally I dared ask, "When did you become a Christian, Marian?" She was silent for a minute and all the exuberance was gone. She asked, wistfully "Oh, Rusty, how do you know for sure you *are* one?" I explained again what she had already heard in Bible study. She gave a sigh of joy, "Oh, then I *am* one!" And I saw again the incredible difference it makes when someone knows who they really are.

I had no idea what was happening inside of Becky as she came week by week to another Bible study, but I suspected it was something pretty big. Once I drove over to her house, but saw that her husband was home, so I went on. Interestingly that very day she had been struggling over exactly how to become a Christian. She felt God pressuring her, almost as if he were in the room. Once she even turned and asked, "God?" because she wondered if he had said something.

She knew that the answer she needed would be in the Bible and so she flipped it open. It fell open at Romans 10 and she read until she found her answer.

If you confess with your lips, "Jesus is Lord," and believe in your heart that God raised him from the dead, you will be saved. For we believe in our hearts and are put right with God; we confess with our lips and are saved. For the scripture says, "Whoever believes in him will never be disappointed."

Romans 10:9-11 (TEV)

She believed in her heart. Then she ran over to her neighbor's, since she also came to Bible study, and confessed with her lips.

When Becky shared her story with us, we

learned that thirteen years earlier, as a young teen-ager, she had gone with a friend to a meeting and heard the Gospel. It was the only time she had ever heard it and she wanted to know God then, but life went on and she forgot. Until her neighbor invited her to Bible study.

Not only will small groups involve you in that kind of follow-up, but it will allow you to share each other's sorrows and joys. In an increasingly impersonal kind of world, we need a small, safe group where we are cared for and understood. Many people live far away from their families or have no close contact with them. A common bond grows out of exercising faith in Christ, even if it is only enough faith to come to Bible study.

I could recite at length the miracles of group care and prayer. I think of the way one neighbor-hood Bible study moved in to support one of their members whose ten year old son had hanged him-self. They even packed up her household and moved the family into a new home. Private hurts and insecurities are healed by group prayer and support. And joys are expanded when someone cares enough to be glad with you.

If your attendance at a small group Bible study is merely a matter of showing up you're missing out—and probably your study lacks a dimension it could have if personal involvement came at a deeper level. We have the example of our Lord in this. He always demonstrated his deep concern for personhood, not just for the propagation of truth. We ought to take more seriously his promise that he would do what we asked in his name. Praying is being involved.

Some years ago we moved to a lovely place in the country. We had found a decrepit old house that needed someone to make it into a home. For a while we found ourselves on the outside, looking in at the community—because we were from "outside," city folks. But eventually I came to know people well enough to begin a Bible study in the area.

One day Geraldine, who was later to become one of my dearest friends, called me on the phone. She lived two miles down the road, and had heard that there was a Bible study in the village and asked if she could come. She came and believed. Her heart was all prepared for the new truths she heard, and her response was one of faith. This was the answer to life that she had been looking for and she wanted to share it with everyone she could. She acted out of deep conviction that Jesus Christ is the answer to people's needs and that life doesn't make sense without him.

I learned a lot from Geraldine, and had many adventures in faith with her. I wish there were space and freedom to tell you about some of them, but primarily I want to share something important I learned from her that I believe illustrates the kind of involvement that makes a small group

Bible study more than another meeting.

My ideal in grocery shopping was to make the interval between the time I entered the grocery store and put the groceries in the cupboard as short as possible. Grocery shopping is not something I enjoy, so I purposed to be as efficient as possible. You see, I really was city folk. Only the small town gave me a tremendous advantage. I never had to wait; I could drive six miles to shop and still cut my time in half.

The problem is that the cultural ways of a small town are different. Going to town means seeing people and visiting. It means having coffee in the coffee shop and greeting friends. I remember stopping briefly one day to chat with two friends who had wheeled their babies down to Main Street to have a coke at the soda fountain in the drugstore. I didn't have time to join them and one teased me, "You're always so purposeful!" I should have caught on then.

One day Geraldine asked me if I wanted to go grocery shopping with her. I agreed to go, and quite unwittingly she taught me what I needed to learn. First we stopped at the restaurant for coffee. In the process of having our coffee, a dozen women joined us at our table, and in the gamut of conversational notes, I heard Geraldine speak with four of the women about all she was learning at Bible study, urging them to come, too.

Eventually we shopped for groceries. I was all

checked out long before Geraldine and did a few errands at other stores in the block while waiting. When I returned, still no Geraldine at the check-out counter. I found her in one of the aisles, leaning on her grocery cart and visiting with a mutual friend. The conversation revealed concern for the total person, and I was not surprised when I heard her ask Gerry where the Bible study met and when, saying she would like to come.

I still don't like grocery shopping and that's not the point of the story. I tell it only to point up that there are things more important than being efficient. When we involve ourselves with people we take on some obligation to sit where they sit and walk where they walk.

I don't know what the cultural pattern is where you live. *You* had better find out what it is, not so it can bully you into a life-style you do not like, but so you can capitalize on its opportunities in your desire to spread the good word about God's love in the area where you live.

New life

"Hey, you guys are getting to me," Ray kidded. "And I wasn't going to let you influence me."

He knew the "guys" weren't what was getting to him and so did they. Ray wrapped himself in a layer of protective intellectualism when he first came to Bible study. They weren't going to con him into anything, he said, and now suddenly he was realizing that he was vulnerable. Something soft inside him was saying, "Yes," to what he was studying.

Bible study is dangerous that way. It is listening to God's diagnosis of man and being forced to agree. It is hearing his solution and having to decide whether or not to make it personal.

A few people sit in Bible studies and seem not to listen, almost as though they have little capacity for spiritual response, whether yea or nay. Most find themselves interacting with truth and being changed. The radical changes come out of personal commitment to Jesus Christ. The loose pieces of life come together and make sense and, as Ray said, "I knew that God must have a higher quality life for me than the one I was trying to live."

The changed life shines out in different ways. One of my friends began wearing bright colors, instead of shades of gray and dark red, and discovered that the world is really beautiful. She began noticing sunsets, blades of grass and birds—as if they had never existed before.

The biggest switch-over involves handing the reins of life over to God and stopping the do-it-yourself projects that kept bringing trouble or stomach ulcers.

One fellow who was in a men's study group told me, "You know what I just discovered? Since I became a Christian, I don't have to be right all the time. It doesn't matter anymore." How blest are those who really learn that lesson!

One of my friends had to learn to have a "quieter voice." She said God gave his verdict on her shrill, nagging tone as clearly as if he had spoken aloud. She saw herself as he saw her one morning while she was praying that her husband would be changed. "God sort of let me know quite clearly that I'd have to change first if I expected him to help with my husband," she said. "And for the first time I saw that it wasn't just *him*, it was *me*. I drive him out of the house with my shrewish ways, and then nag at him for staying away from home so much."

She claimed God's control over her tongue, and it quite discomfited her husband. He missed being nagged at and tried some rather stupid tricks to incite her shrewishness. It wasn't easy to keep cool. Her most frequent prayer was, "Dear God, control my tongue. Keep my mouth shut when it should be, and when I do speak make the words come out gentle." Her husband felt exposed; he no longer had a cover for his selfish meanderings. In fact, he felt guilty. The sweeter she became, the more of a heel he turned out to be.

God didn't just redeem this woman; he redeemed a whole family out of the pettiness of stupid disputes. And he's not finished with the job yet.

The changes in family life delight me the most. I smiled when our son was trying to describe the life-style of a family he had visited. He said, "You remember the way the Murphys lived before they became Christians? Well, that's the way it is at this house."

I knew what he meant. The family didn't eat together; everyone was on his own, raiding the refrigerator and doing their own thing if nothing was ready on the stove. Family members ate when they felt like it; the kitchen was always chaos; the family was out of communication as a group.

When Alice Murphy became a Christian she began gathering her family to sit down and eat meals together—because she wanted the family to learn to thank God for the food. Everything in the Murphy's life took on more discipline and order when Alice started obeying God. Not that families who eat together are automatically Christian—that's just common courtesy, but being a Christian ought to influence our eating and sharing together of the common grace of God.

God even gets to dirty housekeepers. I used to stop by at Eileen's on errands and never got inside the door. That didn't seem a big thing to me until after Eileen became a Christian in our Bible study group. She called me one day and invited me over for coffee. As I walked in she said, "I wanted you to see my house. I've just painted all the walls, got new curtains, and fixed things up. You never saw it the way it was before, but one day I got to thinking that since God lives in me, he lives in our house, and I didn't think it was a suitable place for him to live." Would you believe that her husband and children are also glad God lives there?

Eileen's scene has been replayed many times over the years. God doesn't always insist that a woman love housekeeping, but he has helped motivate many a sloppy woman to tidy things up. Not just for the sake of the house, but because suddenly the people in that house are more important and because these women want to provide an environment that reflects the character of God more adequately. God doesn't overlook dirt and disorder in our lives; it seems consistent that our homes demonstrate this to some degree. For some it may be adding the beauty of a vase of flowers on the table, for others a few trips to the dump—but it seems to be in line with the beginning steps of knowing the Creator, don't you think?

On the other hand, some compulsive over-scrupulous housekeepers have reorganized their priorities and learned to put people first. When they learned to have time for God, they began learning to have time for their family, their neighbors and the church. Many a woman hides from God and the world in her housework and children, seemingly such legitimate places to hide.

One friend, in describing her experience in coming to know God, said, "Would you understand if I said it was as if I always had been living in darkness and suddenly came into the light?"

That's a pretty biblical description of conversion, and I'd like to be able to report that everyone I've seen come to the light in group Bible studies has never gone back to darkness. But that would give a false picture. Some of the most dramatic conversions happen in desperate lives. That very desperation may reveal hidden or obvious instabilities, a lack of inner strength that keeps a person steady. Not all new Christians live happily ever after. And these ups and downs in the lives of group members will be part of the cost of involvement—because they hurt and we care.

I think of one friend whose life God literally transformed. So many bad things in her family life were switched around. An aura of joy settled over the whole family, and the husband was close to wanting to know Jesus Christ himself. But somewhere along the way, when life was at its finest, she blew it. She let go of God and tried doing it on her own, and all the instabilities that had caused the original chaos came in to haunt her and she hit bottom.

Helping group members learn to walk with God is not easy. Hitting bottom doesn't mean you have to stay there, and group encouragement ought to have an elevating affect on all of us. The Bible is full of admonitions about encouraging one another and bearing each other's burdens. When we are born as infants we are put in human families; when we are born the second time with spiritual life, God puts us in the Christian family.

And we cannot underestimate Satan's attacks. The more a group responds to God the harder Satan works to destroy the impact of belief. While he is no small foe, he is not the Victor. In helping new Christians we must acquaint them with the enemy's tactics, but always reaffirm that "he who is in you is greater than he who is in the world." God is still God.

In our personal friendship with group members, I believe three areas of the Christian life need to be kept in focus. I am not suggesting regular sermonettes on each of these subjects, but rather an awareness, an attitude that comes through in conversations as we influence each other.

First of all, the small group Bible study is not the church.

In a day when "organized religion" is out of style in some circles, we need by our personal example and in our conversation to emphasize that the church is important to God—and to us. We need the fellowship of the church, the church's ministry to us, as well as participation in its ordinances. We need pastors and elders to teach and guide us.

Immediately this brings up the problem of the diverse backgrounds of various group members. Some will be no-church, many will be liberal Protestants, others will be Catholic, one or two might be Jewish, others may be members of cultist groups. The question is: when is a church really *church*, as defined by the Scripture? How much should one encourage church which is not biblically *church*?

The small group Bible study is not the place for controversy over churches. The fact that these studies major in what the biblical text says is their strength. Biblical definitions of church will proceed out of continued exposure to the Bible. Since theologians have discussed the above questions for decades without unanimous agreement, we can hardly expect it to be a proper or popular subject for a Bible study group.

Nor do we have to act as church-changers when someone becomes a believer. The Holy Spirit leads people into all truth; if he wants them to change churches let him make them restless. If you are asked privately for a personal opinion, that gives you freedom to say what you believe with sensitivity to the other's position. It has been my personal experience that others observe more than we know about our convictions and church affiliation, and God uses this as he wishes. If there is no church in the other's background, an invitation to yours may be in order, assuming you are happy there yourself. I mention these things because I believe God offers to guide his children as they trust him, and certainly their *family* affiliations are important to him.

A second area of awareness and example is the matter of personal spiritual growth by a daily diet of the right food. Being a Christian is not just believing certain facts; it is sustaining a relationship with God. Relationships demand that time be spent together in communication. The people in the study groups who give evidence of the greatest spiritual growth will be those who spend some time daily reading the Bible. Daily Bible reading isn't some magic talisman to wave over the day; it is having a daily quiet time with the Director of your affairs. Everyone has too much to learn to miss out on daily fellowship with God.

How can you encourage this? By investing yourself in friendship with the members of the group. Sharing ideas you are using will often be a natural part of conversation as you discuss your life with God together. Making helpful materials available also helps interested people.

Learning to pray aloud is a terrifying roadblock to many. Private prayer, yes. But hearing your voice say words to God in front of others can be scary. When the timing is right for the group, perhaps the day you take your turn at leadership will be the right time to suggest that several voluntarily offer sentence prayers of praise to God. If the group likes the experience (and I believe you can talk very freely about whether they appreciated it or not) it could be done regularly and expanded as needs arise. Conversational group prayer is a natural way for new Christians to learn to pray aloud and experience God's presence. In whatever way we can, we want to encourage the idea that talking to God is part of a Christian's life, and above all, that prayer is not making a long speech for public approval.

Friends also share good books. Invest in books that have been helpful to you and pass them along to interested group members. Good books help growing.

The third awareness is both an attitude and a responsibility for communication: it involves the matter of forgiveness. Everyone needs to know 1 John 1:9 and experience it: "If we confess our sins, he is faithful and just, and will forgive our sin and cleanse us from all unrighteousness."

All of us hit bottom at one time or another. We say or do things we know are not right. Our first instinct is to hide from God. Instead, he invites us to come for cleansing so that relationship can be restored. What a gracious Lord!

But hiding comes more naturally than coming for forgiveness, and so we need to be personally aware of this great truth and communicate its good news wherever it is appropriate. The first attitude is a terrible slavery; the second is a wonderful freedom. Walking in the light means being exposed and not being afraid because we are forgiven.

We will need to forgive each other also. People have a way of hurting others, most often unintentionally. In one instance, a person may lash out at others as he feels God's Spirit pressure him. In another, an emotionally needy person may play one member against another. Jealousy arises. Careless words mar the fellowship.

Forgiveness is a Christian reality. God has forgiven us; he forgives us daily for Christ's sake. In view of this, we must be careful not to let our pride keep us from ready forgiveness of others.

Forgiveness is the basis of Christian fellowship.

Contact with God will change you—and everyone in your group who is open to him. Your prayers for group members will be part of your personal investment in the study group. Be ready for some of the most exciting adventures in your life.

Bread

A cold wind had been causing light snow to drift all morning. The snowplows hadn't done their work in our city streets. It was a good day to stay home, and yet here they were—ten women gathered for a Bible study at one o'clock in the afternoon, brought out by some hunger for truth, for a kind of reality they believed possible.

John's Gospel was not an over-read, "old-stuff" document to them. Some had never read it; others had never thought much about it. They were an assorted lot in background, responsibility and religious experience. Some were grandmothers, others had small children, many had teenagers.

A story lay behind each person's presence in the group. It wasn't a *neighborhood* study; it was a group that had evolved out of need and interest.

One person told another or brought a friend. And over a period of years many people had come and gone and been changed.

We were studying John 6 and I was leading the discussion. It is a long chapter with difficult teaching at the end, and I was wondering how the discussion would develop. It turned out to be one of those very special experiences that stay in the memory because God's presence was so real and his teaching so plain.

We had been setting the scene and discussing the miracle of the feeding of the five thousand.

Bread and fish. A mob numbering into the thousands, hungry and milling around on the mountainside. Philip was stewing over how much it would cost to feed a crowd like this, while the more resourceful Andrew scouted out a small boy who had a lunch. "It isn't much," he said to Jesus, "but at least it's something."

We read how Jesus took the loaves and fishes, gave thanks and multiplied it in some divine way so that all the people ate in orderly fashion until they were full. Then Jesus dispatched the disciples to take care of the surplus problem, teaching us something about stewardship of material things.

One woman in the study wondered if this meant she shouldn't throw left-overs away. Another member was curious about what they did with the twelve baskets of food. Did they keep them or give them to the poor? The text didn't say, so the women speculated a bit. It was an alive, eager discussion.

"Of course they wanted to make him king," one woman said, putting down her coffee cup and reaching for another cookie. "That sounds contemporary. People always want to elect the fellow who fills their stomach. Small wonder they were upset when he disappeared. There went their welfare check!"

"But how did Jesus evaluate their interest in him?" I asked. "How did he challenge their value structure?" He cared that they were hungry and so he fed them, but was that the most important thing in life?

We got talking about laboring for bread that spoils instead of working for food that lasts for eternal life. Then one woman observed that the only kind of *work* you could do for eternal life was to *believe* because that was Jesus' answer when the people asked him how they could do God's work. This excited her and she further observed that Jesus talked about *giving* this kind of food—the food which gives life to the world.

Generally I felt the group's reaction was acceptance of this: it was a good deal. These women were ready to say with the crowd, "Sir, give us this bread always."

But we read on. We heard Jesus describe *himself* as the Bread of Life and make an astounding offer. Anyone who would come to him would never be hungry; he who would believe in him would never be thirsty. That sounded like the answer to life's meaning.

"What response does he require?" I asked, anxious to underline the verbs *come* and *believe*.

One of the women commented rather softly, "I guess I've missed out. I'm hungry and thirsty about life all the time."

The others were quiet for a minute. Then one woman ventured, "Did you ever *come* and *believe*? Jesus wouldn't say that if it wasn't true."

Another person exclaimed, "What a terrific offer! It says here that the Father—that's God—draws people to Jesus and Jesus promises never to turn away anyone who come to him."

A good deal of helpful discussion followed, but we were drawing near the nitty-gritty part. Jesus was saying, "I am the living bread which came down from heaven. If anyone eats this bread he will live forever. And the bread which I give him is my flesh, which I give so the world may live."

There was a slight murmur from a couple of people, but the reader went on, " . . . Whoever eats my flesh and drinks my blood has eternal life, and I will raise him to life on the last day. For my flesh is the real food, my blood is the real drink. . . . "

"Sounds like cannibalism," one commented. We finished reading the chapter. A new response was added to *come, believe*. It was *eat*. Bread was all right, but did he have to be offensive? Why add flesh and blood to make it sound so gory? *Come and believe* was such a winsome invitation. Wasn't it enough?

Without saying anything I took a loaf of homemade rye bread from a sack. As I gave it to the woman next to me, I asked the group members to examine it in turn and make any observations they wished as they passed it around the room.

Bread. Brown, rye bread. A swedish recipe. Caraway seeds. Some smelled it. Others handled it as if to weigh it. Several hardly touched it, but passed it quickly on. Bread. Food which we could discuss and describe, to which a price and a nutritional value could be assigned. Bread, brown and heavy, smelling of caraway seeds.

Then it was Sarah's turn. She could hardly wait to get hold of the loaf. She said, "The only way to tell if bread is any good is to eat it," and tore off a hugh hunk from the corner and began to eat. A few handled it as if reluctant to pass it on, obviously more interested than others. Two more women agreed with Sarah. Bread must be eaten if one would appreciate it. Not bread for discussion, but bread for the stomach. It was solid evidence of their commitment to the bread's value.

There, in that warm living room, they were demonstrating the world's response to Jesus. And in some instances, it seemed obvious that the way the individuals handled the physical bread was a good barometer of their hunger for spiritual bread.

Eat. Partake of me, Jesus said. Sarah couldn't learn enough about Jesus. She was a hungry partaker. Others were scared of him, almost as they were of the loaf of bread. Interesting, yes; but pass it on quickly.

We talked then about the cross—the broken body and the shed blood which made the distribution of the Bread possible. We talked about the Lord's supper which symbolizes this. We read again Jesus' words, "The one who eats this bread will live forever."

Some disciples found this too hard. To come and believe and see—that was interesting and profitable. But this kind of close identification, this level of commitment was hard to stomach. Some turned away. And the same thing happened in this room. For some it was asking too much.

Jesus' words were like a piercing sword: "And you—would you like to leave also?" he said to his disciples.

There was a pause. Then one woman, with a shining face and a heart that had grasped the enormous content of Peter's declaration read: "Lord, to whom would we go? You have the words that give eternal life. And we believe and know that you are the holy one from God!"

This has always been the watershed for mankind; it was so in that room. A believing voice said, "Yes, and notice the order of the verbs. You *believe* and then you *know* for sure in your heart. I

used to want to *know* for sure so I could *believe.*
But eating is the proof of the goodness of the
bread."

There it was—a simple Bible study on a snowy
day. Great truth and a loaf of bread. Bread. Come,
believe, eat and know. Jesus said, "I am the Bread
of Life. Whoever eats me will live because of me."

I never read that chapter without all of the
emotion and the mood of that afternoon study
flooding my mind. Sarah had come to the study
by a series of unusual events that God had
arranged. Her attendance was special.

She had studied with Jehovah's Witnesses for
two years, then dropped out because their teaching left her as empty as she was before. In the
interim she had read books, hungered and reached
out for God, and he had brought her into our
group. She later told me, "I knew when I heard
the truth, I would know it *was truth.*"

That day when Sarah ate the bread she gave a
powerful witness to the reality of her faith in Jesus
Christ. Throughout the year and our study of
John, it was often Sarah who had the most pene-
trating insight and always her own conspicuous
radiance.

Summer came and we dismissed the study until
Fall. But before we could begin again Sarah sud-
denly died. It was like an overwhelming un-truth.
Nevertheless, she had died. Thirty-four years old,

three children, dead. All of us struggled to grasp what had happened. Later, Sarah's dearest friend, who had brought her to Bible study said, "Oh, I'm so glad we found this group so Sarah could get ready for heaven."

Personal faith—our entrance into glory.

And it happened in a simple small group Bible study.